Sticky Jam
The Story of Sugar

MEREDITH HOOPER

illustrated by
KATHARINE MCEWEN

WALKER BOOKS
AND SUBSIDIARIES
LONDON · BOSTON · SYDNEY

This is the cane
That grew in the earth
In the sun and the rain.

This is the farmer
Who planted the cane
That grew in the earth
In the sun and the rain.

This is the rat
That hid in the cane
That grew in the earth
In the sun and the rain.

This is the harvester
That cut the cane
That grew in the earth
In the sun and the rain.

This is the train
That carried the cane
Away from the fields
Where it grew in the earth
In the sun and the rain.

This is the mill
That took the cane

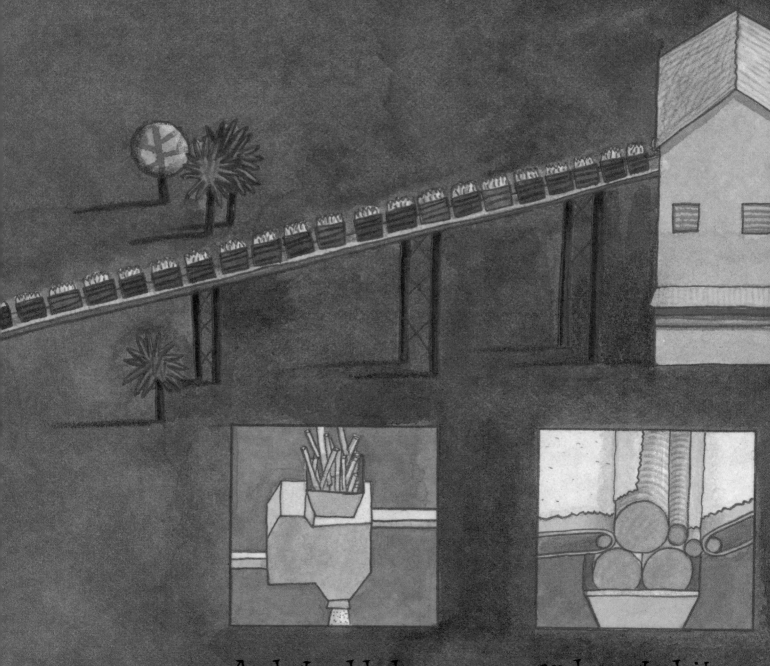

And shredded   and crushed it

And squeezed out the juice

And cleaned   and boiled it

And spun and dried
The millions and millions
Of shiny bright crystals
Of raw brown sugar
That came from the cane
That grew in the earth
In the sun and the rain.

This is the shed
That stored the raw sugar
That came from the cane
That grew in the earth
In the sun and the rain.

This is the ship
Tied to the wharf
Loading up sugar,
The raw brown sugar
That came from the cane
That grew in the earth
In the sun and the rain.

This is the refinery
That took the raw sugar
And dissolved and cleaned it
And filtered and boiled it

And spun and dried
The millions and millions
Of shiny bright crystals
Of pure white sugar
That came from the cane
That grew in the earth
In the sun and the rain.

This is the truck
That carried the sugar,
Bagged into packets
Strapped onto pallets,
That came from the cane
That grew in the earth
In the sun and the rain.

This is the dad
Who went to the store
And bought the sugar
That came from the cane
That grew in the earth
In the sun and the rain

And stirred it
with fruit

And boiled and
cooled it

And put it in jars
As sweet sticky jam.

And this is Harry
Who stood by the field
And looked at the cane
That grew in the earth
In the sun and the rain.

About this book

The sugar cane in this book grows by the sea in Queensland, Australia. Sugar cane is a grass; it likes growing in warm rich earth, with plenty of sunshine and rain.

The farmer uses a special machine to drop short pieces of sugar cane into trenches. Roots push down from the cane deep into the dark moist earth. Shoots sprout up towards the sunlight. The sugar cane grows fast.

When the canes are thick and tall, harvesting machines cut them down and chop them into pieces. The pieces are piled into bins and pulled by a little train from the cane fields to the nearby sugar mill. The cane must get to the mill fast. The sweet sugar juice stored inside the sugar cane must be fresh.

At the mill the pieces of cane are shredded and then crushed between heavy rollers. The brown juice from inside the cane is boiled in big vats until it is thick and syrupy and brown crystals of sugar form. Then the crystals are spun and tumble-dried. The crystals are called "raw" sugar because a few things are still mixed in with the "pure" sugar.

Enormous heaps of raw sugar are kept in storage sheds. From here the raw sugar is loaded into the holds of ships and taken to a refinery to be cleaned all over again. The sugar crystals are dissolved and melted, filtered and boiled, until new crystals of pure white sugar form. The crystals are spun and tumble-dried, ready to be put into packets and sold around the world.

Harry lives near the sea. His dad works in the sugar mill. Harry likes playing on the beach. And he likes watching the little train rattling along its narrow tracks, taking the sugar cane to his dad at the mill.

THIS WALKER BOOK BELONGS TO:

First published 2003 by Walker Books Ltd
87 Vauxhall Walk, London SE11 5HJ

10 9 8 7 6 5 4 3 2 1

Text © 2003 Meredith Hooper
Illustrations © 2003 Katharine McEwen

This book has been typeset in Alpha Normal

Printed in China

All rights reserved

British Library Cataloguing in Publication Data:
a catalogue record for this book
is available from the British Library

ISBN 0-7445-6571-5 (hb)
ISBN 0-7445-8301-2 (pb)